This Book Belongs to:

_____

Thanks to Erika Beckers and Christian Westkemper
for expert advice.

All information, projects, and tips in this book have been carefully
checked by the original publisher, but Abbeville Press is not
responsible for any work done pursuant to this book, or the
resulting products, or any damages. All projects and procedures
should be performed under adult supervision.

First published in English copyright © 2001 Abbeville Press.

Copyright © 2000 Coppenrath Verlag. Text by Susanne Tommes. Illustrations by Thea Ross. Translated
by Laura Lindgren. All rights reserved under international copyright conventions. No part of this book may
be reproduced or utilized in any form or by any means, electronic or mechanical, including photocopying,
recording, or by any information storage and retrieval system, without permission in writing from the
publisher. Inquiries should be addressed to Abbeville Publishing Group, 22 Cortlandt Street, New York,
N.Y. 10007. The text of this book was set in Comic Sans. Printed and bound in Belgium.

First edition
10 9 8 7 6 5 4 3 2 1

Library of Congress Cataloging-in-Publication Data
Tommes, Susanne.
[Waldemar's Grosses Gartenbuch, English]
Wally's big book of gardening / Susanne Tommes & Thea
Ross.—1st ed. p. cm.
ISBN 0-7892-0741-9 (alk. paper)
1. Gardening—Juvenile literature. [1. Gardening. 2.
Plants.] I. Title: Big book of gardening. II. Ross,
Thea, 1949- III. Title.

SB457.T6613 2001
635—dc21   2001022737

Wally's Big Book of Gardening

Featuring Indoor and Outdoor Projects

By Susanne Tommes
Illustrations by Thea Ross

Abbeville Kids
A Division of Abbeville Publishing Group
New York • London

Contents

Hello, Gardeners!

I'm Wally, your gardening expert! I'll be telling you everything a gardener needs to know so that all the plants in your garden, backyard, and windowsill will grow and blossom. Have you ever seen how seedlings grow from tiny little seeds? And then how those turn into real plants with flowers and leaves? It's really fascinating!

Do you want to grow your own plants? This book will show you how to do it, from cuttings, leaves, bulbs, tubers, or seeds. You can grow lots of things in flowerpots or a window box, and then later you can transfer them to a garden—even edible plants like tomatoes, herbs, and strawberries. Yum! Delicious!

Gardening is lots of fun, especially if your friends join you! Do you know anyone who has their own garden? Maybe you can find a patch of soil at school where you can all dig in with spades, rakes, and gloves! Then you can collect plant cuttings with roots from your neighbors and relatives. Just imagine: you often don't need much more than a piece of a leaf to grow a new little plant. I'll show you step by step how to do it!

Have fun!

Wally

What Gardeners Need

Do you want to start a garden on a windowsill, balcony, or outside deck? You'll find useful tools right in the kitchen (but not in the drawer with the fancy silverware!). Ask your parents what you may have.

a shallow spoon to fill pots with potting soil

an old fork with long prongs to loosen the soil

a wooden spoon whose handle you can use to dig into the soil

And if you have your own little flower patch in a garden, then you will also want a small shovel and a rake. CAREFUL: Put on safe shoes so you don't get hurt! Along with these tools, every gardener needs a misting bottle and a watering can with a sprinkler.

To secure climbing plants you'll need a couple of bamboo shoots, a small length of string for tying them, and scissors. With a magnifying glass you can see the buds, blossoms, leaves, and little insects really close up.

You'll also need some flowerpots made of clay or plastic. Plastic flowerpots have lots of advantages: They are inexpensive and sturdy, and they keep the soil moist longer than clay pots since the water doesn't evaporate through the plastic. And you can remove the roots from a plastic pot more easily: Just press in the walls of the pot a little bit.

For very small plants, use egg cartons! Later you can set them right into the ground. Empty yogurt containers also work great. Poke a small hole in the bottom so that excess water will drain out.

If you arrange a layer of broken pottery and pebbles in the bottom of the pot, then the roots won't clog up the hole. Also, when you water the plant, soil can't leak through the hole.

DON'T FORGET TO LABEL!

Clever gardeners collect airtight jars with screw-on lids, which are ideal for storing dry herbs! The jars must be clean and the lids rust-free. For a seed collection, you can use jars without lids. Just stretch a piece of cloth over the top of the jar and secure it with a rubber band—seeds need to breathe!

If you have work gloves and a bright apron, gardening is twice as fun!

What Plants Need

One thing's for sure: Plants need light, air, water, and nutrients. But how much? That differs from one plant to another. Plants that you buy from a flower shop or a garden supply store usually come with a little tag that explains how to care for them. But with or without tags, you'll soon learn what is good for your green friends. Now pay attention!

Light
Plants with small, pale leaves like lots of sunshine. As a general rule, the larger and darker the leaves, the less light the plant needs. However, excessive direct sun or prolonged shade isn't good for many plants. So it's safest if you place indoor plants at a window with a west or southwestern exposure to the sun. A northern exposure is usually too dark, and a southern exposure will be too hot.

Air
Your plants also need lots of fresh air to thrive. So air out your room regularly or—even better—set the plants outside when the weather allows. CAUTION: Plants don't like drafts!

Place in sun. Water frequently, and fertilize in the spring.

Water

When there's been enough rain, you don't need to water plants that grow in a flower bed outside. Their roots absorb the moisture they need from deep underground.

But on hot summer days—and for indoor plants, year-round—you'll have to be the rainmaker. Potted plants will need your help the most, because soil in containers dries out much more quickly than soil in the ground. Here are the most important things to know about watering your plants:

RAINWATER IS A FLOWER'S FAVORITE DRINK!

The best times to water plants are mornings and evenings. It's almost useless to water plants when the sun is beating down on them, since the heat of the sun will evaporate the water before the roots have a chance to drink it in.

Always pour the water onto the soil, not directly onto the plants themselves. Also, it's better to give them a lot of water at once than just a little bit but frequently. The water needs to seep in and moisten all of the soil, not just the surface.

With many plants, however, you may not see any soil at all. So you simply water them by pouring the water in a saucer under the pot. The roots absorb the moisture directly through the hole at the bottom of the pot.

CAUTION: Plants don't like to be sitting in water for too long. So whenever you water them, whether from above or below, take a look a half hour later—if there's still water in the saucer under the pot, pour it out.

If the soil is tightly packed, you'll need to loosen it a little before watering so that the water can seep through the soil and get to the thirsty roots. If a plant has gotten really dried up, set the whole pot into a bucket of water for an hour.

Nutrients

Along with light, air, and water, plants need nutrients. They can usually get it right from the soil. But after a while, it's all used up. So potted plants especially will need more food. You need to fertilize your plants occasionally, but only in spring and summer, which are their growing seasons. But as soon as their flowers have withered, you can't fertilize them anymore, because the fertilizer can damage their roots. There are various kinds of fertilizers available.

BE SURE TO READ
THE INSTRUCTIONS
CAREFULLY!

Liquid fertilizer
for all plants

Solid fertilizer that
quickly dissolves

Time-released
fertilizer that works
for six months

Leaf fertilizer,
good for iron
deficiency

You should also give your plants new soil once a year. Exotic houseplants require special soil from a garden supply store. Native garden and terrace plants are most comfortable in compost-enriched soil. You can make your own compost either as a pile or in a container with a lid and air holes.

When you collect organic kitchen and garden waste to make compost, lots of little animals start to wander into it. Just imagine: In one handful of soil there are more living creatures than there are people on the earth! Many of them are so tiny that you can only see them under a microscope, and so scientists call these microorganisms. Earthworms, pill bugs, and other crawling creatures help them. They all work especially hard when you follow a few rules.

loose, airy
layers of twigs
and straw

organic kitchen
and garden waste

Rule 1: The more varied the food in the compost for the hungry microorganisms, the better the compost will be for the potting soil later. It's making a mixture that counts!

Rule 2: The compost creatures need lots of air to be their best! Twigs, straw, and crumpled paper will keep the compost loose enough for fresh air to get in. Also, use this for the bottom layer so your compost won't get soggy on the bottom.

Rule 3: It's just as important that your compost doesn't get too dry, either. On hot summer days you should spray it with a little water.

If you're using a compost container, put a few shovelfuls of finished compost from your garden pile in the bottom of the container before placing it outside. All the important compost helpers will already be in it—tiny microorganisms, earthworms, pill bugs, and lots of other company.

When the kitchen and garden waste has all been broken down by the tiny helpers, the compost dirt is said to be "ripe." To see whether it's really ready, use the "Cress Test." Here's how it works: In a bowl, sow together cress seeds and damp compost. If the cress sprouts and grows, the soil is ready. And you can even enjoy the tasty cress with buttered bread or in a salad! You can learn more about sowing and yummy herbs on pages 16 and 17, and on pages 20 and 21, too.

Where Do Plants Come From?

Tools, pots, and the very best potting soil—have it all? Then the final thing you need is a couple of plants! Do you want to grow some yourself?

New Plants from Cuttings

HAVE FUN EXPERIMENTING!

Just about the easiest is the spider plant. Their white shoots sprout mini-plants, which you can place right into a pot with soil. In a few days it will sprout roots, and then you can cut it off from the big plant. Spider plants like lots of sun and water.

strawberry-geranium plant

piggyback plant

New plants also grow from the runners of the strawberry-geranium plants. Runners are small vines that the plant uses to spread itself out and grow. Cut the runners off and set them in a glass with water until they sprout roots. Then plant them in soil.
The "babies" of piggyback plants develop directly on the leaves of the mother plants (hence their name!). Let a leaf with a "baby" grow roots in a glass of water.

New Plants from Leaf Cuttings

You can also grow a new plant from just a small twig with a leaf. Remove the twig and set it in a glass of water. Roots will soon sprout, and then you can plant your cutting in a flowerpot.

For some plants, like the African violet, just a single leaf is enough. You can stick the leaf either in soil or in a glass of water. Then it will sprout little roots. And if you place a little piece of charcoal in the water, the leaf will stay fresh. Note: After you've potted the violet, you should keep it warm but not too damp.

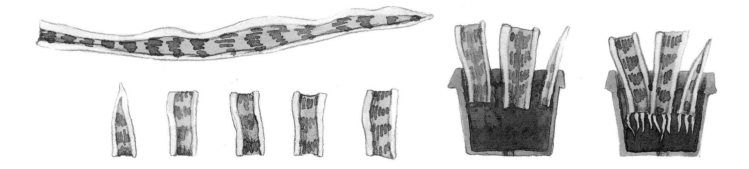

And sometimes just a piece of a leaf is enough! So from a single leaf you can grow lots of new plants. Try it with a sansevieria. Take a piece of leaf about two inches long and let it dry a little before you pot it.

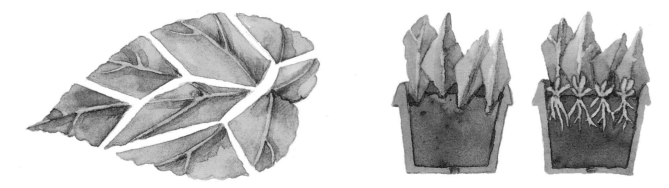

Begonias can also multiply from a single leaf. Just cut a leaf into pieces that still have a part of the main vein running through them, and then plant them with the cut edge down into the soil! With a little luck, roots will soon sprout, and next spring you'll have fabulous flowering plants for your balcony or window box!

New Plants from Rosettes and Roots

It's lots of fun to grow pineapples. You'll need a pineapple, a knife, a flowerpot, charcoal, soil, and sand. Here we go! Cut off the top of the pineapple (with the cluster of leaves) into a cone shape. Rub it with a piece of charcoal and let the rosette dry.

After a few days, plant the rosette in sandy soil, and pour about an inch of fine sand over it. Now you'll need a lot of patience, since there's no guarantee that roots are really growing. But if your experiment succeeds, you can be really proud of yourself!

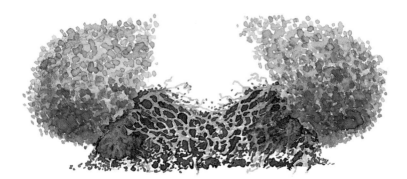

There are even more possibilities under the soil—you can grow new flowers even from the halves of roots! The best time to try this is in the spring, when you can take some roots from plants that you're repotting. The baby's-tears is especially good for this.
TIP: If the leaves turn yellow, just cut off the whole foliage about an inch from the roots. New leaves will definitely sprout soon!

12

New Plants from Bulbs

Imagine this: Inside a bulb there's a whole plant along with all the nutrients it needs to sprout and live. In springtime, the plant makes its way toward the sunlight. When its flowers and leaves wilt, the plant's strength returns to the bulb, and the bulb grows new little bulbs to grow new flowers the following spring. So you need to wait until the wilted leaves are completely dry before you cut them off.

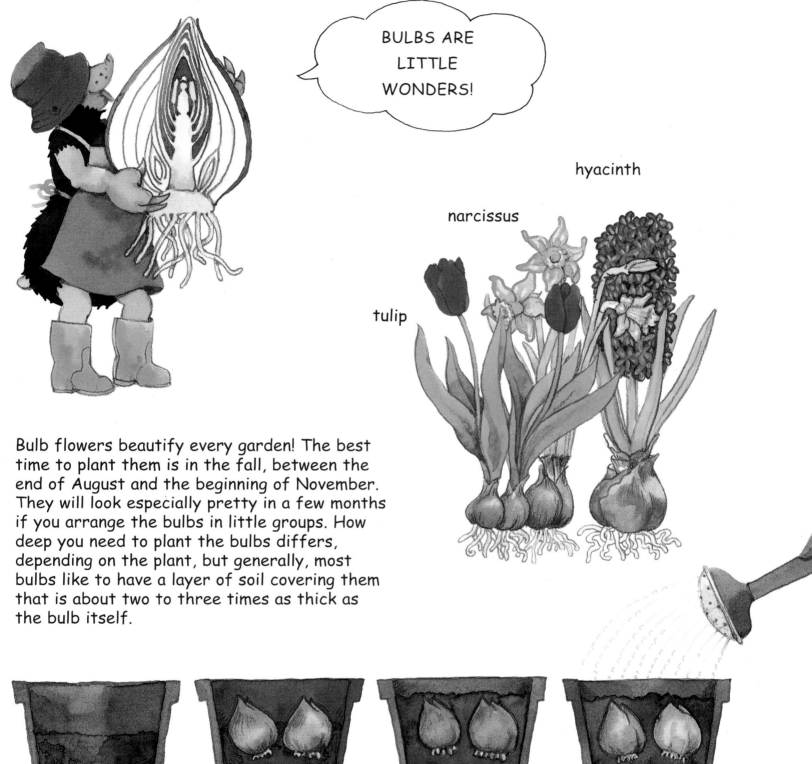

BULBS ARE LITTLE WONDERS!

hyacinth

narcissus

tulip

Bulb flowers beautify every garden! The best time to plant them is in the fall, between the end of August and the beginning of November. They will look especially pretty in a few months if you arrange the bulbs in little groups. How deep you need to plant the bulbs differs, depending on the plant, but generally, most bulbs like to have a layer of soil covering them that is about two to three times as thick as the bulb itself.

Here's how to grow flowers from bulbs on a windowsill. First put a small amount of gravel in a flowerpot and then fill the pot halfway with potting soil. Now embed two or three flower bulbs in the soil, with their pointed end up. Cover the bulbs with soil until the points are just covered up. Water them, and then place the pot in a cool, dark place (such as the basement) for eight to ten weeks. With a little luck, you'll then have gorgeous flowers!

New Plants from Tubers

POTATOES TASTE DELICIOUS—ESPECIALLY FRENCH FRIES!

The best-known tuber is the potato. Its dark spots are actually where new plants will grow! The tuber itself is really only storage for nutrients that the roots take to the rest of the plant. That explains why you sometimes see sprouting potatoes. Plant a sprouting potato in a large flowerpot with sandy soil. Soon it will grow sprouts that turn green before they turn into leaves. Next white or lavender flowers will blossom, and then thick little fruits that look like small green tomatoes will grow from the flowers.

CAUTION: All green parts of the potato plant are poisonous. Do NOT eat them!

Below the ground, the potato you planted will grow new potatoes. In the fall you can dig them up, wash them thoroughly, cook them for about fifteen minutes (with the help of an adult!) and enjoy them with a little butter and salt!

TIP: If you place a potato in a glass of water, you can observe closely how the roots grow!

New Plants from Seeds

Most plants get ready to reproduce as their flowers transform into fruits in which seeds ripen. This is true of pitted fruits (such as peaches, apricots, and cherries), seeded fruits (like apples, pears, and lemons), and legumes such as beans, peas, and lentils, which are seeds themselves in which new plants lie dormant.

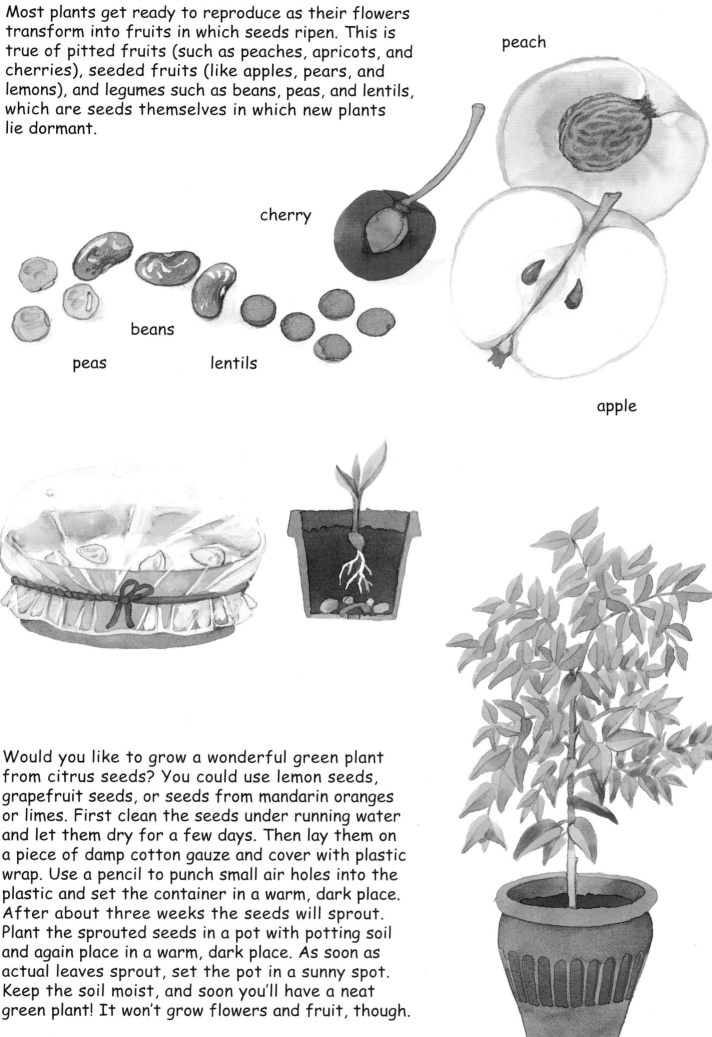

peach

cherry

beans

peas

lentils

apple

Would you like to grow a wonderful green plant from citrus seeds? You could use lemon seeds, grapefruit seeds, or seeds from mandarin oranges or limes. First clean the seeds under running water and let them dry for a few days. Then lay them on a piece of damp cotton gauze and cover with plastic wrap. Use a pencil to punch small air holes into the plastic and set the container in a warm, dark place. After about three weeks the seeds will sprout. Plant the sprouted seeds in a pot with potting soil and again place in a warm, dark place. As soon as actual leaves sprout, set the pot in a sunny spot. Keep the soil moist, and soon you'll have a neat green plant! It won't grow flowers and fruit, though.

New Plants from Kernels

Would you believe that you can grow edible little sprouts in just a few days on the windowsill? Collect some wheat seeds, bean sprouts, mustard seeds, and cress seeds from an organic food store.

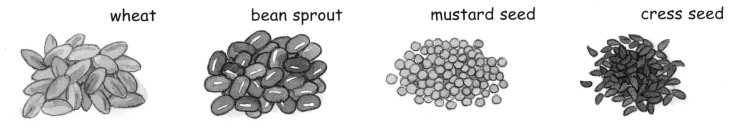

wheat   bean sprout   mustard seed   cress seed

You will also need four saucers and some cotton gauze.

Take each kind of seed and rinse them separately in a sieve with cold water. Moisten the cotton gauze and place it on the saucer. Spread about a tablespoon of the seeds on the gauze. Do this for all four kinds of seed. Cover each saucer with plastic wrap, and make sure to punch a few air holes. Place the saucers in a warm, dark place. Check them every day! Remove the plastic cover as soon as the seeds sprout. Then place in a sunny spot and sprinkle daily with water.

TIP: So you'll always know what's growing where, make a little identification tag and stick it in each saucer!

SPROUTS ARE HEALTHY TO EAT AND TASTE GREAT ON BUTTERED BREAD!

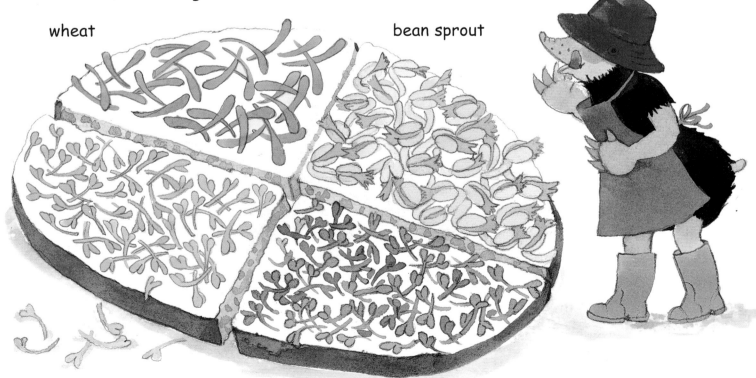

wheat   bean sprout

cress seed   mustard seed

Most kernels are best sown in soil. Here's how:

Fill a pan or a box with soil until it reaches about a half inch from the rim. Spread the soil out flat and sprinkle with water until it's thoroughly moist. Now put the seeds into the soil. **TIP:** Very small seeds are best mixed with sand, which will help prevent too many grains from landing in one spot. Larger seeds can be placed right into flowerpots. Just be careful to place the seeds an inch and a half apart.

Depending on the type of plant you're growing, you may or may not need to cover the seeds with soil. The instructions on the seed packet should tell you. In all cases you should water your seeds at least a little bit. Then stretch plastic wrap with air holes over it. As soon as leaves sprout, remove the plastic wrap.

daisies

Then, when your seedlings are strong enough, you can transfer them to flowerpots, either individually or up to three in a single pot. Gardeners call that "transplanting." Later you can plant your flowers in a larger pot or in a flower bed.

CAUTION: Some plants like sun, and some like shade. The seed packet tells which plants like which.

Beautiful, Bountiful Summer Flowers

With just a few packets of seeds you can turn your balcony and garden into a paradise of rainbow blossoms. You can find mixtures for tall, medium, and low-growing flowers, and even special packets for plants that are especially attractive to bees. Just follow this rule for all annual flowers: Sow in the spring, enjoy in the summer! Remember to cut off any wilted blossoms right away, so your flowers will keep blooming. The instructions on the seed packet will advise you of any special care each individual plant may need. General tips for sowing seeds are on page 17.

Pot-marigolds: Not only do they look great, they're also a time-honored remedy used in ointments.

Snapdragons: For these, it's best to use soil from a garden supply store. Composted soil often contains too many weed seeds—you could get them mixed up!

Sunflowers: These come in large and small varieties. In the winter, birds will come to take the seeds from big sunflowers!

French marigolds: The smell of these outdoor flowers is very strong, so don't plant them too near windows, otherwise that will be the only thing you'll be smelling in your home while the flowers are in bloom! There is also a short variety for potting.

Pretty Climbers

You can also decorate your garden and balcony with climbing plants that will bring forth beautiful blossoms in the summertime. For these you should also read the instructions on the seed packet.

Sweet peas: Before sowing these seeds, soak them for two days in water.

Morning glories: At the beginning of May, you can sow the seeds outdoors. If you do it indoors, move them outside at the end of May.

Pumpkins: In mid-April, plant a couple of seeds in a pot and then transfer them outdoors in mid-May.

TIP: Sow the seeds of climbing plants in front of a fence or a trellis that they can climb up. Or take bamboo sticks and string and build your own trellis for them to climb: Lay the sticks across each other on the floor and tie them together.

You will be amazed how quickly your flowers will bring lively color to a plain outside wall. And as always, remember: Cut off any wilting flowers so that the plant can blossom all summer long!

Yum . . . Delicious Herbs!

Tasty herbs thrive in pots and flower beds, too. Everything you need to know about different herbs can be found on the seed packets or tags. Or simply ask your garden supplier! Some herbs are easy to sow and grow yourself:

Nasturtium is healthy to eat, from flower to stem.
Dill tastes great on fish.
Borage attracts bumblebees.

nasturtium   dill   borage

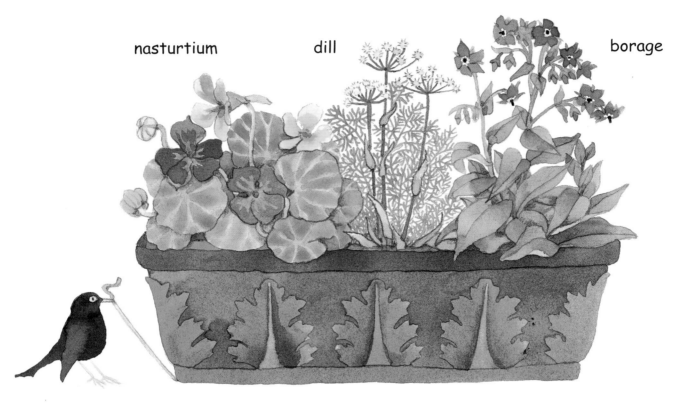

You can collect other herbs as little plants from the market, your garden supplier, or friends.

lovage   chives

parsley   lemon balm

Parsley goes well with all kinds of vegetables.
Lovage seasons soups.

Chives make salads and tomatoes tastier.
Lemon balm garnishes sweet desserts.

Would you like to make tasty herbed salt from your herbs? Here's how: Take the leaves of chives, dill, lovage, and parsley and dry them, grind them into fine crumbs, and mix them with cooking salt. That's it! Your herbed salt will taste especially good on bread with fresh cheese and sliced tomato.

For Mom

For Uncle Kevin

Herbed Salt for Claudia

TIP: Homemade herbed salt makes a great gift! Put some in a pretty container and surprise your friends and family.

You can do even more with herbs. Using freshly picked leaves, you can whip up delicious herbed butter. Here's how: Finely chop a small handful each of chives, parsley, and dill (without the thick stems), and mix them with half a stick of soft butter. Season with salt, pepper, and a splash of lemon. Add a crushed garlic clove, and it will be perfect! Yum, that's tasty!

TIP: Whether freshly picked or dried and used in herbed salt, your herbs can give your soups, sauces, scrambled eggs, salads, vegetables, and even savory breads a really special flavor. Try it!

BON APPÉTIT!

Wally's Vegetable Garden

There are plants galore that you can use to make delicious meals. You can grow many of them right in flowerpots, and the plants on this page are easy to grow from seeds. Read all the instructions on the seed packet first!

Lettuce leaves taste great! All summer long you can pick the bottom leaves to make salads. Be careful, though, not to cut off the "heart," which is the middle piece of the head of lettuce that keeps the leaves growing.

Radishes grow like lightning! In just one or two weeks, green leaves will sprout, and in another three to five weeks you can begin to harvest them. By the way, radishes need lots of moisture. So water daily!

Sugar peas and their soft shells are a sweet treat! Sow them near the end of April, planting this climber in front of a trellis (see page 19). As soon as pods develop, give the plant lots of water! In eight to ten weeks you can harvest the peas.

The fruits of the plants on this page can be quickly harvested if you get them as little plants from the market or your garden supplier.

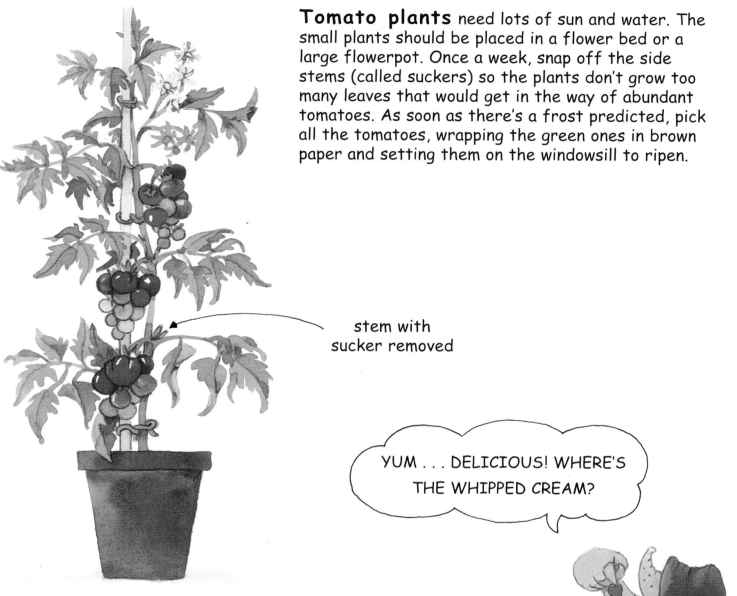

Tomato plants need lots of sun and water. The small plants should be placed in a flower bed or a large flowerpot. Once a week, snap off the side stems (called suckers) so the plants don't grow too many leaves that would get in the way of abundant tomatoes. As soon as there's a frost predicted, pick all the tomatoes, wrapping the green ones in brown paper and setting them on the windowsill to ripen.

stem with
sucker removed

YUM . . . DELICIOUS! WHERE'S THE WHIPPED CREAM?

Strawberries are simply superb—especially with whipped cream! In the first week of May set the little plants outside in a flower bed or in a bucket. However, the "heart" of the plant (the connecting piece between the roots and leaves) must remain uncovered. Strawberry plants love sunshine and damp soil, so water often! As early as July you can try your sweet strawberries.

Plants or Weeds?

Whether a plant is considered a pretty flower or just a weed is only a matter of preference. Weeds are unwanted plants that bother a gardener's lawn or garden. However, other friends of flowers might call these same plants wildflowers and welcome them to grow and blossom. Among these plants are:

nettles

clover

dandelions

daisies

Nettles are particularly distasteful to many people, especially since they prick if you touch them. But nettles are very important to many butterflies. Butterflies lay their eggs on the underside of the leaves, and the caterpillars later feast on these nettle leaves.

Clover is plucked out as quickly as possible by people who like to keep a well-tended lawn. Look closely, because among the many, many three-leafed clovers, you might find one with four leaves. These are said to bring good luck.

Daisies love lawns! There they multiply like crazy and take over all the space for the grass, which annoys many people. But many flower fans love to gather mini-bouquets of daisies.

Dandelions have long roots, which make them really tough to pull out of the ground. Some people can't stand dandelions, while other people love to make salads with dandelion flowers and leaves.

24

However, there are a few plants that almost no one wants to have in the garden, because they take away nutrients and water from the decorative and edible plants. It's no wonder that the sight of them makes many gardeners mad. There's only one thing you can do to get rid of these weeds: pull and pull and pull them out! Also, you've got to keep an eye out and do it while they're still small plants, before they blossom and spread their seeds all over. Sometimes it can help to spread dry leaves on the ground, which can stop the weeds from growing so fast.

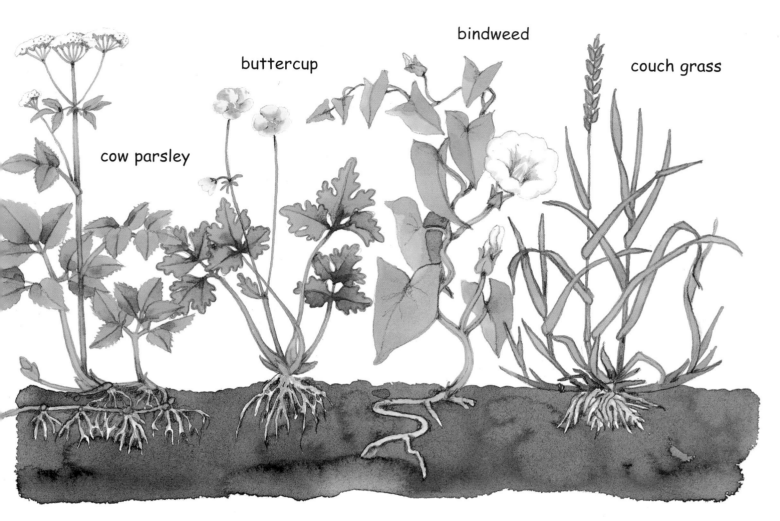

Cow parsley grows profusely near hedges and bushes, but it also likes to spread out in the grass. And wherever it has been just once, it usually remains forever. Its runners are nasty—they can grow as long as almost two feet (half a meter) deep into the ground.

Buttercup likes a home in the garden, whether in a field or in a flower bed. Its runners have strong roots, so the whole plant holds on tight. Buttercup also produces a lot of seeds, which spread very quickly.

Bindweed has roots that are just as strong as well as runners over three feet (one meter) long. They store a lot of nutrients in these runners. If you don't manage to pull the roots and runners completely out of the ground, bindweed will always grow back.

Couch grass is among the most dreaded of weeds. It grows in lawns, in flower beds, and in vegetable gardens. Its long runners sometimes reach over two feet (half a meter) deep in the ground. From each little piece that remains in the ground after you've weeded, a new plant will grow!

Big Little Bugs

If you look at a plant up close under a magnifying glass, you might see a few little bugs, too. Some of them will hurt your green friends, but others can be very helpful.

These are insects gardeners don't like to see:

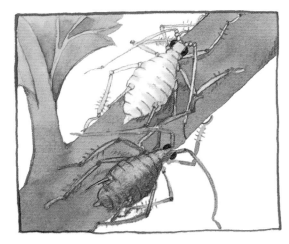

Aphids can be green or black. They suck the leaves of plants and take away their important nutrients. To remove them, mix a little over a quart (one liter) of lukewarm water with a teaspoon (five grams) of liquid soap, put the mix in your spray bottle, and spray the plants with it. You can also fill a pail with water and the soap and wash off plants afflicted with aphids.

Wood lice like damp, dark places, such as under a flowerpot. Too many wood lice can be dangerous because they like to eat up the roots, stems, and leaves. If something seems wrong with your plant, take it out of its pot. If you find countless wood lice crawling on its roots, carefully rinse it off and plant your friend in fresh soil.

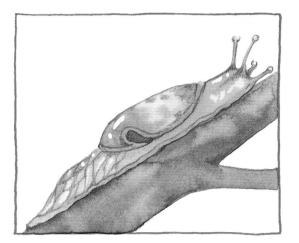

Snails without shells—slugs, that is—like to make homes in your plants. They usually come out at night, so you can collect these creatures in the early morning hours when it's still dark out and put them somewhere they can't do much harm, such as by the curb or in a ditch.

Spider-mites weave a fine web over leaves and suck them until the leaves soon fall off. This often signals that the air is too dry. Cut off any drooping leaves, spray your plant with water, and be glad the next time you see a real spider, ladybug, or green lacewing near your plant, since they eat the spider-mites.

To make sure that your plants don't suffer too much damage, take a critical look at your green friends every day. If you find any damage, it's best to take care of it right away. The earlier you can get rid of these destructive bugs, the better.

There are, however, a few bugs that gardeners like to see:

Ladybugs like to eat aphids. And their offspring, the larvae, find the little crawling bugs especially tasty. Just imagine: One little ladybug can take care of eighty aphids in a single day!

Green lacewings like many little insects in addition to aphids.

Beetles feast on caterpillars, pupa, and sometimes even a snail.

Honeybees, **wild bees**, and **bumblebees** help flowers by pollinating them. Each time a bee visits a flower to collect nectar, some pollen rubs off on the bee's legs. Then the bee carries the pollen to other places. This helps flowers spread out and grow.

bumblebee

wild bee

green lacewing

honeybee

WHAT'S CRAWLING THERE?

two ladybugs

beetle

ladybug larva

pocketbook plant

Cacti: Succulent Survivors

Cacti are very unusual plants: They hardly need water. This isn't surprising, since they come from the desert where it rains so rarely. They have accustomed themselves to a life of desert dryness.

A cactus can store water in its thick stem for a long time, so it can almost always survive a long drought. Since water evaporates through leaves, the cactus has thorns instead. They also protect the cactus from thirsty animals that would love to take a big, juicy bite out of the moist cactus.

Since they are so easy to maintain, cacti are very popular houseplants. They look especially appealing if you place your cacti in a group on the windowsill. A lot of little pots work just as well as a larger container planted with several prickly pals.

bishop's miter

devil's claw

echeveria

living rocks

Here's how to care for your cacti: Just as they are in the desert, cacti like to be planted in sand. Either mix potting soil with clean sand or get some special soil just for cacti from your garden supply store. In their barren native home, the sun is always shining, so look for a sunny spot to place your prickly friend. When the weather's warm, you can put it outside.

In spring and summer, give your cacti a drink of water once a week. So that their flowers will bloom, take care to fertilize them every month with a special cactus fertilizer. In the fall and winter, though, these desert plants need rest. Place them in a cool, bright place (near the window in an unheated spare room, for instance), don't fertilize them, and hardly water them at all. A few drops once a week is plenty enough, believe it or not.

With some cacti it can take an unbelievably long time until you can see that they've grown at all. Sometimes you have to wait a year or even two! Then you need to transfer them to a slightly bigger pot. **TIP:** Put on gloves!

prickly pear

golden barrel cactus

rat's-tail cactus

Trees

You've probably seen a felled tree in the forest. Did you know that from its trunk you can find out how old it is? Inside the trunk there is a ring for each year that the tree grows. Count them and you'll know how old the green giant was when it was cut down.

In the fall, when the days grow shorter and the sun isn't so high in the sky, lots of nutrients are taken back through the tree's leaves. The tree stores the nutrients so that in spring it will have the energy to grow new leaves and blossoms. The leaves also lose their green color, but the red and yellow colors remain, which make the trees really beautiful when the light shines through them. Soon the leaves fall off entirely. If you look closely, you can see little bumps on the branches where they fell off. Tiny buds are hiding there and waiting to bloom next spring.

buds

30

You can even grow your own little tree from tree seeds. In the fall, gather together acorns, beechnuts, maple seeds, and chestnuts that have fallen on the ground. Set them into individual flowerpots (don't forget to write identification tags for each) and cover with plastic wrap punched with air holes. Set the pots on an indoor windowsill and keep the soil in each moist (but not too wet). Now you'll need some patience, but with a little luck, the first leaves will soon sprout. Then you can remove the plastic, and in April or May you can plant your little baby trees outside. Good luck!

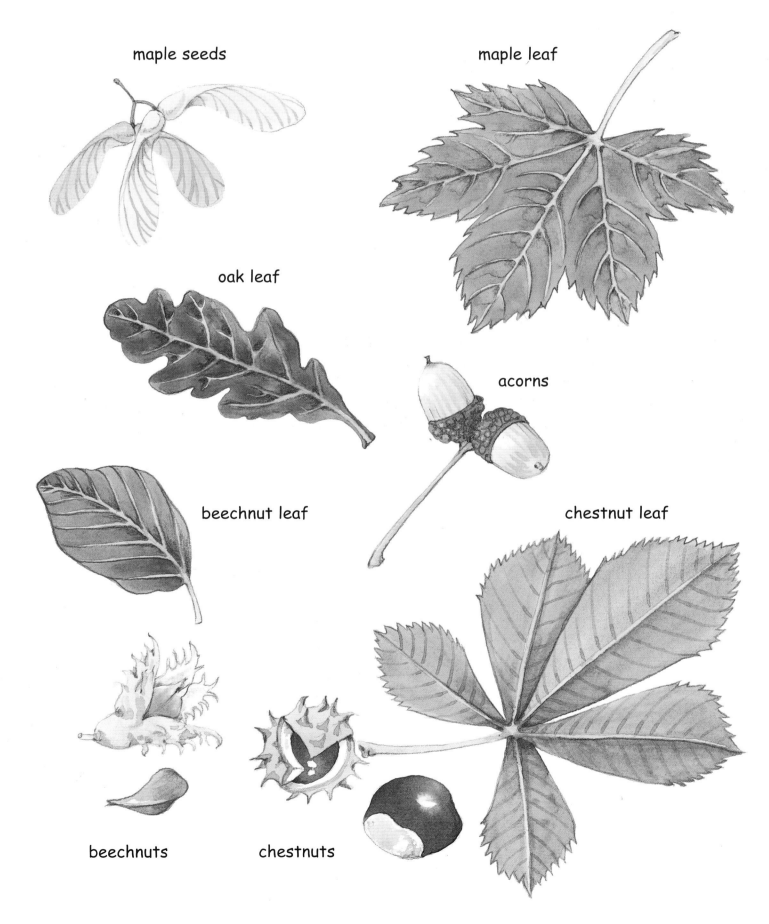

maple seeds

maple leaf

oak leaf

acorns

beechnut leaf

chestnut leaf

beechnuts

chestnuts

Believe It or Not!

Plants That Can Move

Sunflowers, for instance, always turn their flowers toward the sun so they can catch the sun's rays directly. You can see this really well in a field of sunflowers.

Other kinds of flowers move, too: In the morning they open their blossoms, and in the evenings they close them back up. Just watch a tulip!

But some plants, such as evening primrose, are night owls: They open their blossoms in the evenings to release their scent, attracting lots of moths. The moths help pollinate the flowers.

The mimosa is especially sensitive: The instant you touch it with your finger, no matter how lightly, it will immediately pull its leaves together to protect itself.

mimosa

Plants That Eat Insects

Because the ground in which they've grown in the wild doesn't contain enough nutrients, these plants have learned to eat insects. Some larger plants even like the taste of mammals and small monkeys. All of these plants are called "carnivorous," which means "meat-eating." There are many different kinds:

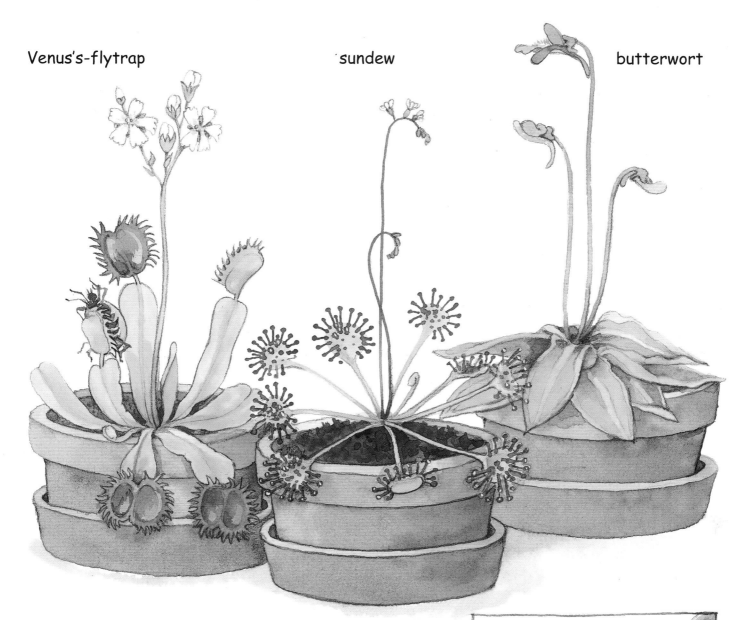

Venus's-flytrap   sundew   butterwort

The **Venus's-flytrap's** favorite food is—this is easy!—the fly. If a fly lands on one of its leaves, the plant will snap the fly shut in the leaf.
The sticky drops of the **sundew** look like dew, and so it attracts thirsty insects. But if they come near, they'll get stuck on the drops and be slowly digested by the plant.
The **butterwort** secretes a sticky substance that insects get caught on. Then the edges of the leaves curve upward and trap the insect in a kind of digesting chamber.
The **pitcher plant** traps insects inside its "jugs." The inside walls are so smooth that the insects helplessly slide down to the bottom, where they are slowly digested.

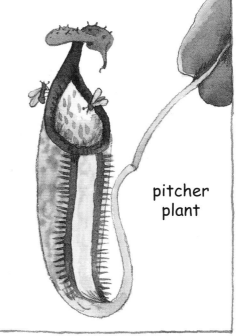

pitcher plant

Plants That Grow on Branches

Plants from the bromeliad family, for example, grow on branches. Want to try to make this happen? The best plant to start with is tillandsia. Get a couple of small plants from your garden supply store, some string, a broken-off branch that divides into separate branches, and a pail with sand. Stand the branch in the sand and use the string to attach the plants to the forks of the branch. To help the tillandsia grow and thrive, spray its leaves in the mornings and evenings with lukewarm water from a spray bottle. If you're lucky, your plants will blossom in the most beautiful colors! Professional gardeners grow many other kinds of bromeliads on branches, too. But they can be a little bit harder to grow, because many have to be secured with marsh moss and require more tending.

Plants That Live between Rocks

You can make your balcony or terrace really eye-catching if you set up a small rock garden in the spring. You'll need a wooden box, gravel, sand, stones, potting soil from the garden supply store, and of course a few plants. Friends and neighbors may even have some cuttings for you. Here's how you do it: Fill the box almost entirely with the gravel and spread sand over it. Now arrange pretty, interestingly shaped stones on top. Crumble the potting soil in the gaps between the rocks, and plant your flowers.

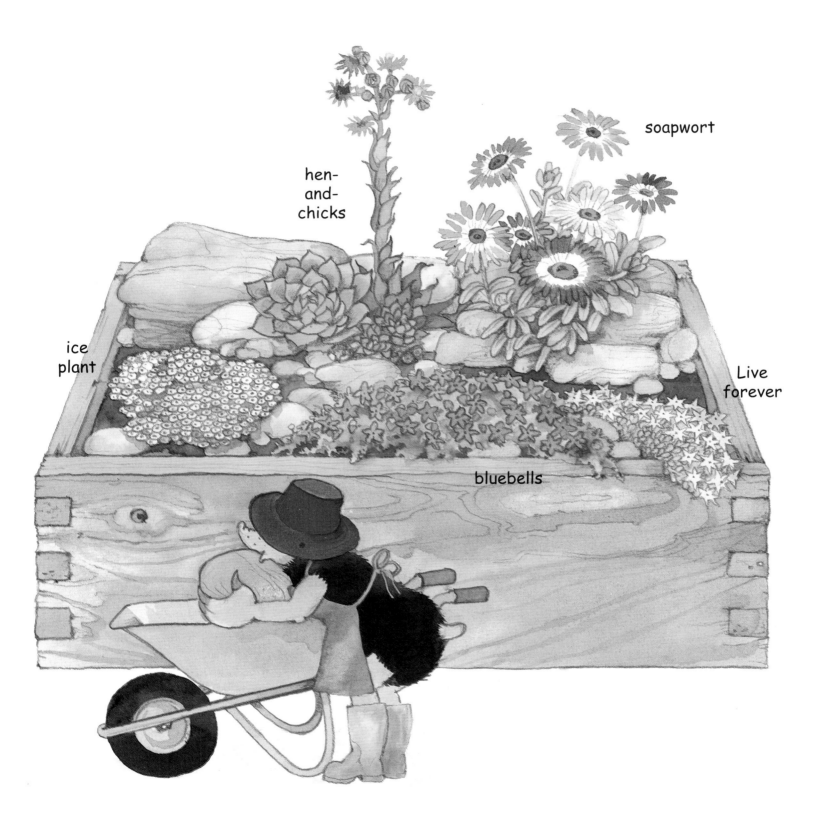

soapwort

hen-
and-
chicks

ice
plant

Live
forever

bluebells

Rock garden plants grow best if you place the box outside in the sunshine. It's important that you regularly water your green friends—but not too much! They don't do well if they stay wet on the bottom for too long.

Plants That Grow in Water

There are plants that spend their whole lives in water, growing in ponds and on riverbanks. Wouldn't it be fun to design your own little pond garden? But you don't need to dig a hole outside to do it. How about using an old tub or bucket, or even a large plastic container?

From your garden supply store you can buy plants suitable for a water garden, such as iris, water lilies, arrowhead, and duckweed. You can also ask for spare plants from any neighbors, relatives, or friends who have a pond.

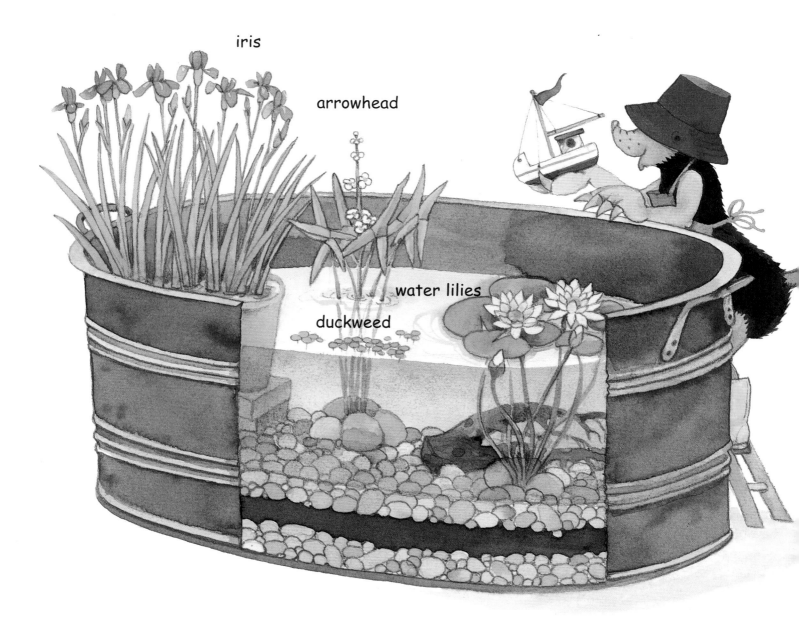

Now you can transform your empty container into a wonderful water landscape. First spread a layer of gravel, then a layer of potting soil, and then another layer of gravel in the bottom of the container, filling it up about one-third. Then you can put in the plants. Set a few stones around the stems so that the plants don't float up when you carefully pour in the rest of the water. Place the duckweed in the water at the very end.

TIP: If your water garden ever grows too full for the plants to have enough room, take some duckweed out, trim back the arrowhead, and separate the water lilies and the iris. You'll surely find someone who'd love to take your spare plants!

As soon as your water landscape is set up, keep a watchful eye out. It won't be long before a few little creatures come by to take a look at your "pond."

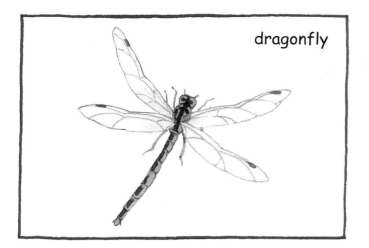

dragonfly

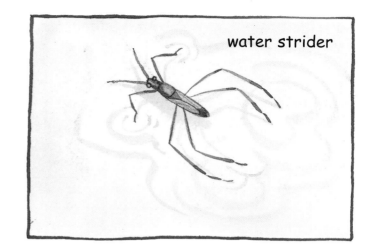

water strider

Has a dragonfly shown up? Or has a water strider scooted across the surface of the water?

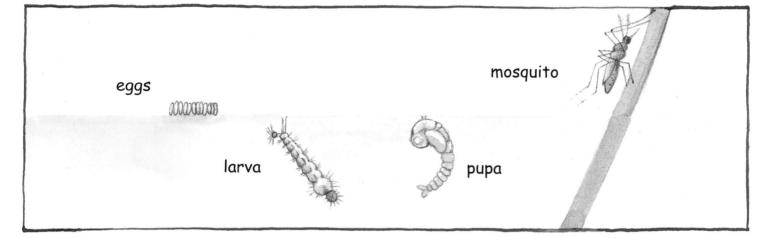

eggs

mosquito

larva

pupa

You may also see a few mosquitoes, who lay their eggs on the water. From their eggs hatch larvae, which hang onto the surface of the water with their heads facing down. About four weeks later the larvae become pupa. Then something fantastic happens: After just two days, a grown mosquito crawls out of the pupa's hard shell and climbs to the surface of the water! There they dry their wings and soon fly away. Interestingly, only the female mosquitoes sting, because they need the blood to lay their eggs.

Especially curious nature researchers can fill a glass with some water and look closely at it with a magnifying glass. You may spot water fleas and water beetle larvae. Have fun experimenting and observing!

water fleas

water beetle larva

What Do I Do in Each Season?

Gardeners are busy year-round. Here is the most important work that you need to keep in mind:

Spring
(May and June)
- As soon as there's no more danger of a frost, place all house plants—including cacti—outside.
- Start to water cacti more often (give them a drink every week).
- Fertilize house plants and cacti.
- Plant little trees outside.
- Sow summer flower seeds, climbing plants, cress, dill, borage, lettuce leaf, radishes, and sweet peas.
- Plant parsley, lovage, lemon balm, chives, strawberry plants, and tomato vines.
- Set up rock and water gardens.

Summer
(July and August)
- Since it's usually very hot during these months, water all plants generously. Plants in pots or tubs that are placed outside in the sun should get a good drink of water every morning and evening.

- Keep the compost pile moist.
- Tie climbing plants to a fence or a trellis.
- Regularly cut off wilted flowers from your summer flowers or climbing plants.
- Snap off the foliage stems (suckers) from tomato plants.
- Harvest herbs, lettuce leaves, radishes, sweet peas, strawberries, and tomatoes.
- Refertilize house plants and cacti.
- Cut away wilted foliage from bulb flowers.
- Don't forget to weed!

Fall
(September to November)
· When frost is a danger, bring house plants and cacti back inside.
· Give house plants and cacti a rest by placing them in a bright, cool, but frost-free room until next spring.
· Don't fertilize, and water less.
· Pick tomatoes, and wrap in paper any that are still green, allowing them to ripen on the windowsill.
· Trim down plants that have grown too large.
· Cut back summer flowers and climbing plants. Gather their seeds for sowing next spring, store the seeds in glass jars, and toss the rest of the plants on the compost heap.

poppy

· Gather the seeds of large sunflowers, bring them inside, and spread them on a plate to dry.
· Collect acorns, beechnuts, maple seeds, and chestnuts, and plant them in pots.
· Plant flower bulbs in the ground.

Winter
(December to April)
· Feed the hungry birds with sunflower seeds.
· Water your cacti only a tiny bit every week.

39

Index of Plants and Insects

YOU CAN FIND MORE GREAT
GARDENING INFORMATION
IN THE AMERICAN
HORTICULTURAL SOCIETY
ENCYCLOPEDIA OF
GARDENING.